GET IT OUT!

Get It Out!

Dream, Create and Make It Happen

Christal M.N. Jenkins

DEDICATION & ACKNOWLEDGEMENTS

This book is dedicated to all of the dreamers and those who dare to dream bigger.

To my husband: thank you for always dreaming with me!

To my family: continue to see that which God entrusted to you come to pass.

To my son and god children: never lose your imagination! Don't allow anyone to kill your dreams! Work hard and make them happen!

Special thanks to Brooke Brown, Anna Miller and Tina Bruce. I love you all dearly!

TABLE OF CONTENTS

PREFACE

As I was thinking about having to teach an upcoming workshop on "Self-Publishing", I began to contemplate on what I would say to those eager writers looking to have their wonderful work shared with the world. I had to think about my own journey. I was challenged with the notion of how to inspire others when I had not been faithfully following my dreams or been diligently using the gifts God has given me. I felt compelled to write this book in that moment. It came out like a flood of words being skillfully laid out by God's design. He wrote every word and I was His instrument. This book convicts my heart and challenges me to never give up on my dreams.

By no means have I walked out everything in this book. However, I am now taking the necessary steps to walk it out. I can empathize with those who get stuck and want to give up at times. Our creative ideas, dreams and gifts are given to us to use and put into action. They are not meant to lie dormant in our minds. I hope and pray that this book challenges and inspires you that no matter what happens in your life you can still fulfill your dreams. Time waits for no one but time is also a gift. We must not waste it! We must make every minute count!

For those of you who no longer dream, I want to encourage you to dream again! Life is too short to spend it wondering what could have been. You can make it a reality now!

Greatness is in front of you. Stop waiting on others to motivate you! GET IT OUT and Make It Happen!!!

Always,
Christal M. N. Jenkins

Get Up!

As I sit here and write, the words "Get Up!" ring loud in my mind. I challenged myself to decide to either sit here and dream or get up and do it! Like many of you, I have dreams that are entertained only in thought. The very thought of the dream becoming a reality can best be described as a devastating tantrum of disdain for the process it will take to see it through. The process of seeing dreams become a reality discourages me from even beginning.

Now I must pause for a moment to briefly explain what I mean by dreams. God, ultimately, is the giver of our ideas and dreams. When He gives them to us He is trusting us to carefully and responsibly manage them. If your idea or creative vision will hurt or bring harm to people, animals, or the environment, it is safe to say that it is not a God given idea. Our dreams are meant to produce good fruit; to edify and enrich the lives of the world in which we live.

I am well aware of what I have been entrusted to steward. I have been blessed with the ability to bring life to words, ideas, dreams and concepts through writing. Even though this is my gift, I still struggle with putting my dreams into action.

This is a book written for dreamers by a dreamer. I have come to realize that it doesn't matter how grandiose your dream is or how small your idea may be. The point is you have something special that needs to move from your head-space out into the real world. The longer you allow it to re-main dormant, the longer you will be restless and struggle with trying to pretend that it is only a dream that will never come true.

It is crazy to think that I, too, still struggle with releasing my dreams into the atmosphere. I have seen many of my dreams come to pass right before my eyes. But for some strange reason, every time one is realized and a new dream approaches I get slow footed and afraid. I find myself catch-ing a case of the "what ifs". I am sure you can relate. You may think, "What if people think my idea is stupid?" or "What if no one wants to read my book?" or "What if I can't get the money I need to make this happen?" Then the "what ifs" turn into the "I can'ts". "I can't write as well as _____". The downward spiral continues and turns into the "I don'ts". "I don't have the time to do this" or "I don't need other people critiquing me" or "I don't want the pres-sure that comes with being in the spotlight".

Every time we go down this path our words bring death upon our dreams. One day you will wake up and realize that the only reason it never came to pass was because you killed it!

Don't you think that if God Himself entrusted you with a dream that it is your reasonable service to steward it? You were chosen by God to see it through. He wouldn't have blessed you with it, if He didn't equip you with everything you need to accomplish it. He is rooting for you! He has complete faith in you to accomplish this goal! Don't give up on your dreams! Make them happen! The choice is yours. Not using your gift will feel like you are carrying around dead weight. It will inevitably drag you down. Don't waste any more time with the "what ifs", "I can'ts", and "I don'ts". When you get up the only words you should be telling yourself is "I CAN!"

FAILURE ISN'T FINAL

One Sunday morning I was sitting in church. My mind was going around in circles about my current life circumstances. Fulfilling my dreams and purpose was the last thing on my mind. It was in the midst of my overwhelming thoughts that I heard the pastor make this declaration: "failure isn't final". Hearing those words felt like a huge burden was lifted off of my shoulders. For the first time in a long time I felt a sense of freedom from my past mistakes and failures.

In the past, when I experienced failure, I believed the lies that told me "this is the end", "it is over", and "I will never recover from this one". These lies are so funny to me now because I realize that it is never the end or over with God and I always recover. Recovery may not look or feel the same way every time, but I have found that God gives us the ability to be resilient. Being resilient means that when you fall you get back up, dust yourself off, and keep on going. How many times in your life have you messed up? If I kept a count, it would be way too many to even list. The truth is we mess up all the time, but an even greater truth is that we can get up every time! What if we lived our lives focused on our goals instead of our mistakes? What if we lived our lives with the faith to see things through and not allow our failures to hold us captive?

It is very easy to let our failure handicap us, paralyze us, and keep us stagnant. The worst trap is when we make subtle moves in the same spot somehow convincing ourselves that we have moved in another direction. When in actuality, we are still in the same place where we fell. Your will to move has to be combined with your ability to do so. You can't just wish you could be doing better, you have to do better! I can't wish I could exercise every day and then come home and lie in the bed and watch TV. My will without my determination to accomplish the task will never cause me to do anything.

I have spoken to so many dreamers in my short lifetime. Many of them will never even put those dreams on paper, let alone act on them. Every time I see them I brace myself for the long conversation about what they "shoulda", "coulda", "woulda" done. My philosophy is if God is still breathing breath in your body, then you still can accomplish that goal. It is not too late!

Living in the midst of your failure is just an excuse to not move forward. You are afraid to become the better you, the "you" God envisioned. You are afraid to fail again.

Guess what? Once you move forward you probably will fail again! This is how life works!

What is wrong with continuing to go forward in spite of your failure? I do not want my life to be governed by my failures but instead by my ability to be resilient and press on. When we fall we have to assess what happened and see it as a great opportunity to learn and grow. No matter what people may say, you build strength every time you get up again!

You have heard the saying: "It doesn't matter how many times you fall, it matters how many times you get up!" I am not dismissing the fact that failure may come with severe consequences. Yes, we have to be held accountable for our actions, but accepting our consequences and rectifying our wrong doing is a part of getting up and moving forward.

The truth is that we cannot control how others will respond to our growing pains. But, why are we worried about that in the first place? Our primary focus should be on what we need to do to move forward. You have to do your work first. You cannot expect others to do it for you or follow after you. If you do the work you need to do then you are positioning yourself back on the path of success. Allowing other people's mindsets and words to negatively impact you will only make you a slave to their actions. You are free to be who God is molding and shaping you to be. You are not bound by anyone else's opinions of you. Yes, people's opinions should be taken into reflective consideration, but they should not determine whether you get up and move forward! Only you can determine that!

Your failure is a part of your life. It is a moment in time and it is something that we should all learn and grow from so that we can move forward. It does not put a period in your story! Don't allow it to keep you from accomplishing your dreams! Allow it to be motivation to continue to push you forward despite the obstacles that you may have faced. Stop dwelling on your past. No one can run forward when their head is turned backwards. They will most likely fall and hurt themselves. So keep your eyes on what's ahead of you.

Think of your life as a boxing match. No matter how hard you fight you keep getting knocked down. The good news is that in a boxing match, if the bell has not rung, the fight is not over. In the midst of the fight your failure may seem fatal, but it is not FINAL!

Do or Do Not. There is No Try!

remember being in Mr. Patterson's 8th grade math class at Wy'east Jr. High where every morning he would make us read a quote from the many that adorned the top of the walls in his class room. There are many that I still remember and apply in my life to this day. One of them is so befitting to discuss with you. He had a quote that read "*Do or do not. There is no try. -Yoda*". Now I was not a huge Star Wars fan, but that quote resonated with me. There is no such thing as trying to do something. Either you are going to do it or you are not. How many times have we said or heard someone say "I am trying". In our minds we know it is not true. "Try" is a word we use to get people off of our backs. It is a word we say to make us feel better about not really achieving or accomplishing anything in our lives. We say "I am trying to do better", or "I am trying to pay attention", or "I am trying to be a better____ " (you fill in the blank).

We have to make up in our minds that we are no longer going to try, we are going to do! The minute we come to that resolve the only choice we have is to get up and move forward. Have you ever heard a person say "I am trying to quit smoking" while they are holding a cigarette in their hands? I am sure you are probably laughing at this example, but that is my point. How silly does that person look? Their actions and their words are a contradiction. Either they are going to quit or they are going to keep on doing it. There is no in between.

As human beings, we are so clever. God has created us with such great intelligence and we sometimes use its power in an adverse way. Instead of doing what we know we are supposed to do, we use our intelligence to think up lies and excuses about why we haven't done it. Strange, but so true! Sadly, many of us have convinced ourselves of the very lies we so eloquently spew out of our mouths. We believe them as truth. When we are confronted by others, we get defensive and combative because we are so offended that someone would dare to call our bluff.

The truth is, you know that deep in your heart you are wrong. The very root of your "truth" is a lie. A lie when faced with the truth will always be exposed as a false sense of reality. If we are honest with ourselves, much of how we govern our relationships, engage in our daily work, and conduct our lives is based on lies we have told ourselves for years. So much so, that we use the excuse "this is just who I am" to cover them up and make them appear real. Those lies are NOT who you are and they never were. At some point in your life, you got caught up in the "try" cycle and never stopped. So you are left with not accomplishing much of anything.

I know some of you think that you are accomplishing your goals but really you are just doing busy work. Busy work makes it appear as though something is actually getting done. Think about how much time you have wasted in life "trying" to do something instead of just doing it. In the same way, using the phrase "I'm going to" is just as bad. I have heard so many people say what they are "going to" do and never do it. Case in point, "I am going to go back to school" and six years later they haven't taken more than one class. The problem is they have traded their will to do with an excuse not to. If you listen to that excuse long enough, you will begin to believe the lie and live out a false sense of truth as your reality. Days, months, and years will go by and you will look back and wonder where all the time went.

Even in scripture, James admonishes us to be "Doers of the word and not hearers only"[1] and states "Faith without works is dead"[2]. If we do not "Do" we are doing nothing. It's harsh to think about it that way, but that ultimately is the truth.

Stop "trying" to do! It only makes you run in place and never advance. If you run in place long enough you will just be kicking up dirt and digging yourself deeper into a hole. The only way you are going to see your dreams become reality is to DO!

THE WILL TO DO

Sometimes we forget that God has equipped us with everything we need to accomplish our goal. God gives us both the creative ideas and the will to do them. We just need to tap into that will more often. We should constantly be using our will in our lives but many times our will sits on a shelf waiting for us to grab hold of it and use it. Your idea isn't meant for you to figure out what to do with it. God is waiting for you to get it out and exercise your will to see it to completion. Your "will to do" requires you to have faith in God and not in your idea. If we place our faith in our idea then we can easily lose hope and sight of the end goal. Our idea is not the end goal, it is only the beginning. God knows the true purpose for what this idea will flourish in to and become. We have faith in God because He was the one who gave us the idea in the first place. He manufactured it and we need Him to show us how to use it.

Maybe your faith is a little faint. You find it difficult to see God in this way. You may believe God exists, but you feel as though you have gotten this far in life by your own ability. I do not want to be the bearer of bad news, but your ability to "do" was given to you by God before you were even born. He saw fit to enable you to do everything that you are currently doing. No strings attached. God is not a God that says, "If I do for you, you have to do for me". He does for us ungrudgingly, which should motivate us to respond to Him with our faith.

The problem with placing the emphasis on our own abilities is that even though they are God given they are limited by our own humanity. Therefore, our abilities can falter and are not reliable all of the time. As humans we get tired, distracted, and change our minds. If "we" become the focus then we look to our own abilities to accomplish the goal. Therefore, we set limitations on what our dreams can truly become. The sky may be your limit, but God holds the universe. I don't know about you, but I want more than just to reach the sky. I want everything God has purposed for my life and dreams to become reality.

Furthermore, our humanity makes us fearful of the unknown. So by the mere fact that we are human, we lack the ability to trust what we can't see. That is where true faith comes in. Faith enables us to trust God for what we can't see and believe that what we have hoped for will come to pass. Our will to do is more than human manufactured willpower. It's a supernatural ability to grab hold of our dreams and accomplish them.

What is it that you are holding on to? What idea did God entrust to you? In order for it to move from just being a dream, you must exercise your "will to do" through faith. Faith in God is a sure thing! It will not fail you! We may fail, but God will never fail us!

We must see our creative ability as inseparable from our will to do it. Therefore our dream is never separated from our faith and our will to see it through! If God gave it to you it has to come to pass!

You Can Do It!

Have you ever found yourself in a place where you had no one around to encourage you? I have been there on many occasions. You don't need to wait until someone encourages you to get up. You just need to encourage yourself. Some days I have to look at myself in the mirror and say: "Yes you can do this!" "You are more than equipped to handle this!" "Don't give up no matter what! You will see it through until the end!"

Our faith in God says, "I am not alone in this and He has my back". It invigorates us and strengthens us to be able to do what we were entrusted to do. You may have heard the scripture "I can do all things through Christ who strengthens me"[3]. Notice the word "ALL". With God as your strength there is nothing you cannot do!

ALL means ALL! So from this day forward do not ever tell yourself "I can't" because you can! Do not tell yourself

"I am not able" because you are! God is not attempting to pump your head up just to see you fail. That is not how He works.

Faith in God simply put is about believing that He is who He says that He is! So if He says that in His strength you can do all things, then, guess what? You can! It is funny to me that I have heard this scripture for over 30 years and yet I forget the power that these words possess! "I can do all things through Christ!"[4]

We should not base our ability to see it through by the size of our idea. Isn't that usually how it goes? We will determine whether or not we want to rely on God's strength depending on how crazy we think the idea is. No matter how we rank our God given creative ideas on our scale, we will always need His strength to complete them.

You are not in this alone! Don't stress and worry by putting unnecessary pressure on yourself! Don't talk yourself out of it before you get started!

You have all the encouragement you need to take the next step. You have His strength backing you up. You can do this!

GET IT OUT!

Many of us have never allowed our dreams to see the light of day. We keep them imprisoned in our minds. You have to get them out of your head. By getting them out of your head, you are giving them life. Our words either speak death or life[5]. We have the power to choose.

In Habakkuk 2:2, God tells him to "write the vision". There is a freedom and a release that comes when that which was held up inside finally comes out. Most of our anxiety, stress, and strain exists because we continue to hold it in. So it plays in our minds over and over like a song on repeat. We can't shake it or focus on other things because it always finds its way back to the surface of our minds. Why do we allow what was supposed to be a blessing to become torment? We continue to torment ourselves by not releasing our vision.

You may be thinking "I don't have it all thought through yet, so I am just waiting until I get it all together in my head".

Can I help you with something? You can probably speed up the process by beginning to write down the little bit that you have now. I guarantee you that it will start to form and become something even greater than you imagined.

What is the harm in getting it out of your head? Some people may say "if I tell someone they may steal it". Yes, that is a possibility, but what if you allow your God given discernment to lead you to the person God intended for you to share it with all along? For some of you, it is just a matter of getting it out on paper first. This will free your mind to be able to progress in thinking about the next steps.

Our minds are so powerful and we must use them to be a temporary storehouse for our ideas and not a permanent residence. You may think that you are limited by your daily schedule. If that is the case, maybe you should re-evaluate how you spend your time. I have heard it said that God gave us 24 hours in a day and if we needed more He would have allocated more time. God has provided us with enough hours in a day to accomplish what we need to for that day. In your assessment of your time you may find pockets and windows where you can be creative to dream and release your thoughts.

It may be while you are driving to work; You can record your thoughts on your mobile device. It could happen during a lunch break just jotting down notes on a post-it. It doesn't matter what you use to capture your dreams you just need to get them out of your head.

This is the first step in bringing life to them and seeing what was once a creative idea come to fruition. So stop keeping it a prisoner in your mind and get it out!

Fail To Plan, Plan To Fail

Benjamin Franklin once said, "If you fail to plan you plan to fail". Every dream must have a plan. You have to know how you are going to accomplish this goal. The plan will outline the steps you need to take. It provides the blueprint to your creation. I know we want to do all of this in our heads but it is just not possible. We must layout our ideas and organize them so that we can ensure that we understand what we will actually do.

How you draft the plan is up to you. Whether you use a template, or just create a simple outline with basic steps. Depending on what you are attempting to create, you may need to consult someone or do research on how to accomplish the tasks necessary to complete the goal. We live in the information age where everything can be accessed at our finger tips. There are no excuses for not taking the time to do the work needed to ensure that you have a plan in place. There is nothing wrong with having a plan. It will not slow down your process. If anything it will help you move forward more efficiently.

The reason many dreams never see fruition is because of lack of planning. We tend to want to skip this step and just get to the "doing" as if planning is not a part of the "doing" process.

In Proverbs 16:9, Solomon writes "a man plans his ways but God directs his steps". It is important that we make a plan. It holds us accountable to what we were entrusted with. It reminds us of where we are going and where we have been. It is a guide to our next stepping stone and light to shine down our path.

Imagine if an architect envisioned a beautiful house and drew the exterior design but did not create a blueprint and just started building it. How would the construction workers know what to do? How would they know the measurements for laying down the foundation? Where would the walls and support beams need to be placed? How large are the rooms in the house? Can you imagine how long it took for them to even construct the final design? I am sure you can visualize what that house ended up looking like when it was done. Nothing was placed where it was supposed to be. It turned out nothing like what the architect had envisioned.

In Habakkuk 2:2 it says not only to write the vision but to make it plain. The message version puts it this way. "Write what you see. Write it out in big block letters so that it can be read on the run". The bottom line is that the plan has to be clear. It needs to be clear so that you know what your vision really entails and you can share it with others.

It May Take More Than YOU

Did you ever think that the vision or dream God gave you wasn't just for you or about you? Most of us are very narcissistic in our thoughts about what God entrusts to us. We must use caution when we say things like "What God has for me is for me!" Because many of us do think it is all about us. I hate to burst your bubble but you getting up and moving forward to accomplish your goal is almost always connected to someone else.

Look at it this way; each of us are given pieces to a puzzle. Every piece is designed to be connected to another piece. You hold a piece that someone else is waiting on. I know some of us think of ourselves as a "jack of all trades". But we were not created to do everything by ourselves.

It doesn't matter what the project is, you will need someone to come along side you to help you accomplish your goals. You may be the dream bearer but seeing the dream come to fruition doesn't just begin and end with you. You have been entrusted with the idea but there are other parts to the dream becoming reality that may come from some else. However, you won't know that if you keep it to yourself. I cannot tell you how times I have heard testimonials from people that when they shared their idea it ignited a fire in others and they wanted to know how they could support their vision. What was just a small idea in someone's head is now a huge creative reality in the form of an organization, business, building, book, group, conference, etc.

Don't selfishly harbor your idea. You need to share it with those who you know God has placed on your heart for you to share it with. They are waiting on you! They have what you need to see your vision become great! Don't lie to yourself and think that you have to do it all alone. Remember it is His idea that He has given to you, so your role is to be a good steward and not a prison guard.

God has already positioned people to support you and protect your vision as it is going through the process. They are an integral part to how your idea will be planned out and executed.

If you don't know of anyone else, pray and ask God to show you who they are. You may have to wait a little bit but if they are a necessary component to your idea coming to pass God will send them. Don't allow fear and your need to control hinder what God desires to do through this unified work. Make sure when they come you remain open to what God has purposed for you all to accomplish.

PATIENCE IS A VIRTUE

So here you are. You have made a conscious decision to get up and move forward. You have released your idea from your mind, made a plan and have also connected with others. Now what? My mother used to always say, "patience is a virtue". Sometimes things happen right away. I love life when it happens that way. But truthfully speaking, it can take a while.

Our faith is tested when we have to wait to see it through. It is in the waiting period that we can find ourselves doubting our ability and the abilities of others. It is in the waiting period where we can find ourselves getting discouraged and wanting to give up.

I will never forget when I wrote my first book, "<u>Discovering the True Love Within</u>". I had never written anything like that before and I had decided to self-publish it. I figured once it was published on all the major distribution channels it would just sell itself. Over time, I became discouraged because I wasn't seeing the results that I had expected. I would think thoughts like, "everyone knows it is available now, why aren't they buying it?" "Is it not good?" "What did I do wrong?" The truth was that I needed to not only continue to promote and connect with others but that it was all in God's timing. What do I mean by that? In the process of writing, publishing and promoting that book, God was working on me. He was preparing me for the platform I am walking on today. Little did I know, what was to come. I never thought I would publish another book or even co-author a third book. But God knew all along.

You see, in my head I had thought that the idea God gave me to write a book was all that I had to steward. I thought I just had to get it published and I was done. All along, God was using that as a means to prepare my life for something greater. Maybe you are reading this book and you are in the waiting phase. You had such high hopes in the beginning but now it seems like nothing is happening, or maybe all you are getting is closed doors and you find yourself in a hallway contemplating what to do next.

Be encouraged that even it if takes a while your vision will come to pass. There is so much more that you may not recognize happening behind the scenes. God is crafting a masterpiece and all you see is the part that you were entrusted to create. Your vision was purposed and destined and will bring life. It just may take some time. It doesn't matter what it is, everything has a timeline. DON'T GIVE UP! The worst thing we can do is give up too soon. So often people come so close to their breakthrough, and give up right when they are about to reap their reward. Don't let that be your story. You have to see it through!

In some cases, maybe you need to re-assess the short term and long term goals of your idea. For others, maybe you need to expand your vision and dream bigger. Whatever the case may be, you have to remain encouraged and focused on seeing it come to pass. You have come too far to quit now!

Look at it this way, the Bible says 1,000 years is like 1 day to God. Wow! Use your spiritual imagination with me. What if God had planned for your vision to go to the next level in 50,000 years and you stopped at 49,000? You would have given up one day short of seeing it come to fruition. Only God knows the ultimate timeline for things to happen in our life. Trust Him in the process. Don't rush the wait because you want to make sure that you are ready when it is go time!

I quoted Habakkuk 2:2 in an earlier chapter, but verse 3 really drives home why we should be patient and wait. I love the way the message version says it:

"This vision-message is a witness
    pointing to what's coming.
It aches for the coming—it can hardly wait!
    And it doesn't lie.
If it seems slow in coming, wait.
    It's on its way. It will come right on time.'"[6]

You can be encouraged in knowing that it may "seem slow", but "it's on its way. It will come right on time"!

Beware Of The Killers

'm sure many of you know of someone who is a dream killer. Dream killers lack the ability to achieve their dreams so they spend their time kicking up dirt on others and suffocating the life out of their dreams. If they are not accomplishing their goals they do not want to see anyone accomplish theirs either.

It is also possible for you to be your own dream killer. Every time a dream comes to your mind, you quickly kill it with your words. You downplay the idea and suppress your creative ability. These actions make you a dream killer. You have to wonder if you are willing to kill your own dreams, what are you doing to the dreams of others around you?

Why would you want to kill your own dreams? Maybe you kill your own dreams because you are only focused on supporting someone else's dream. Yes, we may be called to support someone else, but at some point you will have to fulfill your own dreams. Your dream could very well be tied to their dream, but if you stop dreaming while you are supporting their dream then you will never know.

Interestingly enough, dream killers can be bigger than just individuals. They can be an environment, a culture and/or the society that we live in. The American culture kills dreams every day. We teach kids to be more rational and less imaginative, as if having an imagination is immature. It is this kind of thinking that limits our creative ability and numbs our natural desire to want to create.

Much of the technology we love to enjoy came from a creative idea in someone's mind that they shared with someone else and together that dream is now something we all can enjoy.

Don't allow yourself, people, or our society to kill your dreams. You must protect your ideas and see them through. There is greatness inside of you waiting to come out and be shared with the world.

Sure your idea may seem small, but scripture reminds us "do not despise small beginnings for the Lord rejoices to see the work begin."[7] Do not let the size of your ideas deter you from accomplishing your goals.

Allow your dream killers to motivate you and not aggravate you. Only you can control what you allow to stop you.

You have made enough excuses already! Don't allow dream killers to be your excuse for not fulfilling your dreams. You have to say to yourself, "You can attempt to ridicule my idea, squander my strategic plan or trump my next steps, but you can't kill my dream!"

Dream Again!

Maybe you are reading this book and you are thinking that there was a time in your life where you did dream, but you stopped dreaming a long time ago. You convinced yourself that since none of your dreams ever amounted to anything it wasn't worth it to spend your time dreaming. The truth is that you are not alone. There are millions of people who feel that very same way.

Many have even traded their dreams for someone else's. God created you to dream; to have creative ideas and to create the very things you have dreamed up. Think about how the universe was created. God had a creative vision and He used His will to create it. The same goes for us. We were made in His image and in His likeness. We possess the ability to be creative and to create! Our dreams are what we were created to do. What if Thomas Edison decided his ideas were stupid and wanted to give up because he wasn't able to make them work? We would not have the electric light bulb, music players or cameras.

Most of us think someone else will come up with it someday and they can do it. If God wanted them to do it, He would not have given the idea to you. You cannot stop yourself from dreaming. To do that would be inhumane and unnatural. Your purpose and destiny is anchored in your ability to creatively dream and do! Living out our purpose is what fuels our passion in life! If we are not living out our purpose we are like the walking dead, existing but not doing anything of value.

We were created to have value and to share value. My question to you is, "if not you, then who?"

Today Is A NEW Day

Today is a new day! It is God's gift to you—breath and life. You are here today not by mistake but by God's plan. No matter what happened to you yesterday, you have to shake it off and move forward today. Yesterday is behind you and no one is promised tomorrow. Today is all you have to work with. Make the most of it. Don't allow this day to slip by. You have purpose in you, waiting to meet your destiny in front of you. Don't wake up today and begin to put limitations on yourself!

No more "what ifs", "I can'ts", "I don'ts", "I'm trying to", or "I'm going to". The only words you need to say to yourself are, "I can and I will do!" You have everything you need to get up and see it through. Challenge yourself today by getting your dream out of your head. Make a plan to see it through and follow it.

What are you waiting for? All of your excuses have been used up. Time waits for no one and you have wasted too much of it! Today is the day you say "I CAN" and then you "DO!"

Placing your faith in your Creator, speaking life to the ideas He has given you, and putting action to your words will guarantee that your life will never be the same again. "Your best days are in front of you" is not just a cliché, it is the truth!

So what do you say? Are you going to allow today to be the day you come alive again? Are you going to dream bigger than you ever have before and become everything God envisioned for you to be?

God's strength is supporting you. His purpose is inside of you. His destiny is before you. His goodness and mercy will follow you and His grace will lead you. What do you have to lose? The choice is yours, so make it a good one! Don't give up on your dreams, GET THEM OUT and MAKE THEM HAPPEN!

ENDNOTES

Scripture References

i   James 1:22 NKJV

ii James 2:26 NKJV

iii Philippians 4:13 NKJV

iv ""

v   Proverbs 18:21 NKJV

vi Habakkuk 2:2-3 MSG

vii Zechariah 4:10 NLT

Other Books by the Author

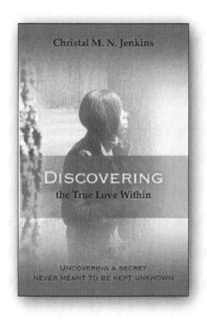

Made in the USA
Columbia, SC
21 June 2022